The Mental Capacity Act and 'Living Wills':

a practical guide for Catholics

The Catholic Bishops' Conference of England & Wales
Department for Christian Responsibility & Citizenship

The Catholic Truth Society
Publishers to the Holy See

The Mental Capacity Act and 'Living Wills': a practical guide for Catholics. The Catholic Bishops' Conference of England & Wales - Dept. for Christian Responsibility & Citizenship, 39 Eccleston Square, London SW1V 1BX.

Published 2008 by the Incorporated Catholic Truth Society, 40-46 Harleyford Road, Vauxhall, London SE11 5AY.

Front cover image: *Stethoscope* © John Wilkes Studio/CORBIS.

The Keeping Faith series

This publication is part of a series which aims to assist in addressing the pastoral needs of Catholic patients and to provide pastoral, theological and practical guidance for Catholics and other Christians in healthcare in England and Wales.

Other publications available:

Caring for the Catholic patient - A guide to Catholic chaplaincy for NHS Managers and Trusts – 1 86082 417 X (Do 748)

Caring for the Catholic patient – Meeting the Pastoral needs of Catholic patients – 978 1 86082 418 0 (Do 747)

Contents

Foreword

By Archbishop Peter Smith

"I have come so that they may have life, and have it to the full" (John 10:10)

As Christians we believe that every human life is a gift from God and that to live that life fully we must love one another. Illness, whether mental or physical is a part of the human condition and most if not all of us will have to cope with it at some time in our lives. Ill health makes us aware of our human frailty, and calls for a response of love and care, recognising always that to be human is to be body, soul and spirit, and that we are ultimately called by God to follow Our Lord through death to the fullness of life with Him.

This Guide seeks in a practical way to bring this Christian perspective to bear on a number of difficult questions arising in new legislation - the Mental Capacity Act - which came into force in October 2007. The Mental Capacity Act is about all the practical choices that have to be made on behalf of people who cannot make some decisions for themselves. These may be financial decisions, choices about where to live, or how someone is to be cared for. It is the healthcare concerns, viewed in the light of Catholic moral teaching, that are the main focus of this booklet.

The Mental Capacity Act did not come out of the blue. For several years, patient groups, lawyers, and others had argued that a new law was needed in this area. But when a first draft was published there were justified anxieties. Rather than empowering and protecting people in the area of end-of-life decisions, some of the original proposals appeared to seriously threaten them. Lawyers raised anxieties about the new attorneys who seemed free to bring about someone's death by refusing life-sustaining treatment. Doctors were concerned that, because of rashly-made advance decisions, they would be forced to stand by while patients died from neglect. Groups representing vulnerable people saw inadequate safeguards, fearing the new law could legalise euthanasia by omission.

For the sake of the common good, many people including the Catholic Bishops of England and Wales took an active part in the debates over the draft bill. On several occasions the bishops proposed changes to improve the safeguards in the bill. A number of these changes were accepted by the government. A vital provision was inserted into the Act to make clear that it did not change the law prohibiting euthanasia or assisted suicide. A further crucial provision made explicit that no-one acting on another person's behalf can take a decision motivated by a desire to bring about a person's death. But whilst the Act passed by parliament contains many important safeguards such as these, there are still some problematic features with the new law.

This is new and complex legislation and we will of course want to keep under review how this Act works in practice, and whether any aspects of this Guide may need to be revisited in the light of experience in the years to come. Whilst this legislation is particular to England and Wales, some of the moral questions raised by this Act are new and will be of significance for Bishops' Conferences in other parts of the world where similar legislation may well be enacted.

This Guide seeks as practically as possible to answer many of the questions which you might have about this Act in relation to healthcare decisions, whether it concerns your own future, that of a friend or a member of your family who may be seriously ill, or whether you are a healthcare professional. We have not tried to cover every eventuality but rather to set out considerations which we hope will be of assistance to those working out how best to act in particular and sometimes painful and difficult situations.

This Guide is designed both to be read through, and also to be a point of reference on a specific question. Therefore certain important points are repeated so that as far as possible individual sections are complete if read in isolation.

I would like to thank the working group which has produced this Guide - Dr Clare Walker, Guild of Catholic Doctors; Dr Catherine Gleeson, Consultant, St Catherine's Hospice, Crawley, Fr Paul Mason, Principal Chaplain Guys and Thomas' NHS Hospital trust and in particular Professor David Jones, St Mary's University College Strawberry Hill, who has done the lion's share of the drafting. Over the summer of 2007 we published a draft of the Guide for consultation and I would also like to thank the very many individuals and groups who kindly took the trouble to respond and comment on the draft. In particular I would like to thank the National Board of Catholic Women for their very substantial and detailed contribution.

Although the Guide rightly focuses on the practical issues people face, for Christians these of course find their true context within the Gospel message of hope. As Christians we are called to a vision of life and love beyond illness and even death itself. With that in mind, Cardinal Newman's prayer may help us to keep that vision in our minds and hearts especially when faced with difficult decisions.

O Lord
Support us all the day long of this troublous life
Until the shadows lengthen, and the evening comes,
And the busy world is hushed,
And the fever of life is over and our work is done.
Then, Lord, in thy mercy
Grant us a safe lodging, a holy rest,
And peace at the last.
Amen.
(Cardinal John Henry Newman)

Whatever your own situation, I hope you find this Guide to be of help.

+ Peter

Archbishop Peter Smith
Archbishop of Cardiff
Chairman, Department for Christian Responsibility and Citizenship
February 2008

1 Introduction

1.1 About this booklet

The Mental Capacity Act 2005 specifies how, according to English law, decisions should be made on behalf of people who do not have the capacity to make decisions for themselves. The parts of this law dealing with advance decisions ('living wills') and lasting powers of attorney came into force in October 2007. The Mental Capacity Act is about all the practical choices that have to be made on behalf of people who cannot make some decisions for themselves. There may be financial decisions that need to be taken, or choices made about where to live and how someone is to be cared for. There are also all the day-to-day choices that have to be made - what we do and do not want to eat, for example. The Mental Capacity Act also covers healthcare decisions made when the end of life is approaching, and these decisions understandably cause people particular anxiety. It is the moral issues surrounding such healthcare decisions that are the main focus of this booklet.

The Mental Capacity Act aims to ensure that people are given a rightful say in their own care in advance of a time when they may be unable to make a particular decision for themselves and to clarify what a carer can reasonably do on behalf of someone who is not able to make a particular decision. For several years, patient groups, lawyers, and others had argued that a new law was needed in this area.

The Mental Capacity Act clarifies the way a person can make his or her wishes known in advance. It also introduces important safeguards into the law. For example, it lays down that an advance refusal of treatment must be written and witnessed and must be valid and applicable to the situation. It also specifies that, in relation to life-sustaining treatment, a decision about what is in the 'best interests' of the patient must not be motivated by a desire to bring about death.

On the other hand the Mental Capacity Act is far from perfect. It is still the case that a doctor may be prevented from acting in the best interests of the patient where there is a valid and applicable advance refusal. Furthermore, the Catholic Church holds that providing food and fluid by tube is part of basic care but the Code of Practice accepts the view that 'artificial nutrition and hydration' is medical treatment which may be withdrawn. Neither of these disturbing features was newly introduced by the Mental Capacity Act. They were already present in case law and medical practice.

The present guide provides a Catholic perspective on the new law and how we should act now that it has come into force. This guide is for you if you want to plan for a future when you can no longer make decisions for yourself. It is also for you if you are responsible for the care or treatment of an incapacitated adult.

- The guide first gives an overview of the Mental Capacity Act.
- It then explores the issue of withdrawing or refusing medical treatment at the end of life, acting in someone's best interests and the new powers in the Mental Capacity Act to make advance decisions and to appoint proxy decision makers (lasting power of attorney).
- This guide sets out what possibilities the Mental Capacity Act gives for people to plan for the future, and guidance on making these choices effectively and morally.
- It includes specific guidance for health and social care professionals in relation to the implementation of the Mental Capacity Act.
- The guide concludes by providing sources of further information and assistance, advice on writing statements of wishes and feelings and on making advance decisions to forego medical treatment.

1.2 Summary of key points

The purposes of the Mental Capacity Act 2005 are first to enable individuals to make their own decisions as far as possible and, second, where this is not possible, to empower others to act in their best interests. The main provisions of the Act enable you to appoint one or more people called attorneys to make decisions in your best interests should you be unable at some time in the future to make decisions for yourself. The attorney may be appointed to make decisions about Finance and Property, or Health and Welfare. This is done by means of a legal document called a Lasting Power of Attorney.

According to the Act, you can authorise your Health and Welfare attorney to make decisions in your best interests about refusing or withdrawing life-sustaining treatment but you do not have to do so, and if you do not give the attorney this authority, he or she cannot take such decisions.

The Act also specifies that you may make an advance decision to refuse treatment. If this includes a refusal of treatment which may be necessary to sustain life, in order to comply with the law it must be signed and witnessed.

The Act makes further provision through the Court of Protection for situations where someone lacks capacity to appoint an attorney, or has not done so.

The Act requires that all decisions be in the best interests of the person lacking capacity. It also requires those caring for the person to take reasonable steps to consult anyone named by that person about what would be in his or her best interests.

In relation to decisions to refuse medical treatment some people are more concerned about the danger of under-treatment and the neglect or even the starvation of some (especially older) patients. Others are more concerned about the danger of over-treatment and the potential of modern medicine to make the dying process needlessly burdensome. It is important to take account of both of these concerns.

It is sometimes right and just to allow illness to take its natural course even if this means you will die. There are two aspects that need to be kept in mind here: cherishing life and accepting death. Cherishing life entails that death should not be the aim of our action or of our inaction. On the other hand, accepting death entails that we should not flee from the inevitable by seeking unreasonable treatment to prolong life when such treatment is likely to be futile.

Not everything allowed by the Act is morally the right thing to do. For example, refusal of food and fluids is morally unacceptable (when death is not imminent) unless they can neither provide nourishment nor alleviate suffering, or cannot be taken without really significant physical discomfort.

When planning for a time when you cannot make decisions for yourself, it is good to talk with someone you trust, who may be a friend, a family member or a priest. If you are thinking about making an advance decision to refuse treatment you should also talk to a doctor. If you are thinking of making a lasting power of attorney then it might be sensible to get informed legal advice.

It is important to bear in mind that particular healthcare decisions depend on many factors and cannot be reduced to following a set of rules. A prerequisite of good practice is a positive ethos of care within the healthcare setting. Without a supportive environment, decisions may be made insensitively and people may be in danger of under-treatment or over-treatment.

2. What is the Mental Capacity Act and how could it affect me?

2.1 What is it aiming to do?

The Mental Capacity Act aims to provide a statutory framework to 'empower and protect people who may lack capacity to make some decisions for themselves', for example, people with dementia, learning disabilities, mental health problems, stroke or head injuries. It seeks to clarify who can take decisions in which situations and how they should go about this. It also aims to enable people to plan ahead for a time when they may lack capacity.

2.2 What are its 'key principles'?

The Act is based on five key principles which also guide how the Act should be put into practice. The key principles are:

- *A presumption of capacity* - every adult has the right to make his or her own decisions and must be assumed to have capacity to do so unless it is proved otherwise;
- *Individuals being supported to make their own decisions* - a person must be given all practicable help before anyone treats him or her as not being able to make his or her own decisions;
- *Unwise decisions* - just because an individual makes what might be seen as an unwise decision, he or she should not be treated as lacking capacity to make that decision;
- *Best interests* - an act done or decision made under the Act for or on behalf of a person who lacks capacity must be done in his or her best interests; and
- *Least restrictive option* - anything done for or on behalf of a person who lacks capacity should be the least restrictive of his or her basic rights and freedoms.

Among these five, the first and fourth principles seem to be the basis of the others: to enable individuals to make their own decisions when they can and, to act in the best interests of those who lack capacity. These "key principles" of the Mental Capacity Act should be interpreted in the light of basic moral principles as taught by the Catholic Church. For example, in a Catholic understanding the "best interests" of the patient includes those interventions that provide for a reasonable hope of benefit, including the benefit of life itself, without imposing excessive risks and burdens on the patient. This guide aims to help people interpret and apply these key principles in an ethical way.

2.3 What possibilities does the Mental Capacity Act give me to plan, in case I lose capacity in the future?

There are several things the Mental Capacity Act allows you to do to prepare for the future:

- To make known your wishes and feelings, and identify the people you wish to be consulted should you lack capacity to make specific decisions;
- To authorise people to make decisions in your best interests through setting up one or more lasting powers of attorney; a Health and Welfare attorney can act only when you lack capacity; a Finance and Property attorney may act at any time you choose;
- To make an advance decision to refuse medical treatments; if this concerns life-sustaining treatments the Act further specifies that the decision must be in writing and must be witnessed.

It is important for your family, future carers and for the people you have chosen to make decisions for you that you make your wishes clear. You can do this by writing a statement of wishes and feelings. There is advice on how to do this at the end of this Guide. It would also be important to discuss these matters with your family, your carers, your doctor, your priest and where relevant your solicitor.

2.4 Are there issues that I need to think carefully about?

There are several issues you need to think about carefully: What would be the risks and benefits of granting a lasting power of attorney for Finance and

Property? What would be the risks and benefits of granting a lasting power of attorney for Health and Welfare? Who should I choose to act as my attorneys? How will they cope with this responsibility? Do they understand my wishes and feelings? What would be the risks and benefits of making an advance decision to refuse treatment? Should such an advance decision include possibly life-sustaining treatments? Will it prevent doctors or nurses from giving me the treatment they think is in my best interests? How can I help the healthcare staff to give me the treatment I need and want, and not to give me treatment I do not need and do not want? Reading this booklet is one way to help you think about the issues. As you read you can think - how would this affect me? Is this an issue for me? Other places to find useful information are given at the end of this booklet.

It may be helpful to make a *written statement of wishes and feelings* that could guide those who may have to make decisions for you. They will be helped if they know what matters most to you and what you are most concerned about. Advice on writing a statement of wishes and feelings is provided at the end of this booklet.

It is also a good idea to name one or two additional people who should be consulted when decisions are made on your behalf, whether about financial and property matters or about personal care. These people do not have to be relatives. They can be friends or carers. The Mental Capacity Act requires healthcare professionals to make reasonable efforts to consult the people you have named.

People who are consulted when a health or care professional is making a decision about what is in a person's best interests are likely to be asked if the person previously expressed views about how they would like to be treated or about their approach to other similar situations or relevant beliefs. The named people are not being asked to make the decision themselves, nor are they being asked for their own opinions.

Having written a statement of your wishes and feelings, or an advance decision, you should go back to it from time to time to see if you still agree with it, or if you need to update the named person or persons to be consulted. You should think how people would find these documents:

a copy could be held by your GP and copy kept at home. Perhaps a copy could be kept by a friend.

2.5 Who can I talk to if I have questions about planning ahead?

It is good to talk about planning ahead with someone you trust, who may be a friend or family member, a priest or a nurse or doctor you know well. If you intend to make an advance decision, you should also talk to your GP, and perhaps to a solicitor. He or she can tell you what the consequences might be. If you are thinking of appointing someone with a lasting power of attorney then you need good legal advice, because lasting powers of attorney can be drawn up in different ways.

2.6 How does the Mental Capacity Act affect me, if I am caring for a relative or friend?

Unpaid carers, friends and relatives will need to know their responsibilities to help the person in their care have a say in that care. They will also need to know what they can reasonably do for the person in their care if that person cannot make decisions.

2.7 How does the Mental Capacity Act affect me, if I am a health or social care professional?

The Mental Capacity Act requires health and social care professionals to know what they can reasonably do when looking after someone who cannot make decisions about their own care. It also reinforces a person's right to make decisions for himself or herself if he or she is able to. As a paid carer or a health or social care professional you have an obligation to familiarise yourself with the Act and the Code of Practice which goes with it. There is a provision in the Code for healthcare professionals who disagree with a decision in relation to life-sustaining treatments not to have to act against their personal beliefs, as long as they do not simply abandon the patient or cause their care to suffer. (Code of Practice, 9.61)

3. What does the Mental Capacity Act say about healthcare decisions when life nears its end?

3.1 Why are people anxious about withdrawal of life-sustaining treatment?

Every human life is irreplaceable. It is important that we cherish every life, including our own, even when life is difficult or is near its end. The life of someone who is sick or dying or disabled must be respected no less than the life of someone who is healthy. One reason that people are anxious about withdrawal of life-sustaining treatment is because they fear that sick people will be neglected and not be given the treatment they need. This is called under-treatment. Even if this neglect is at the person's own request, it may be because the person fails to value his or her life.

3.2 Why are people anxious about receiving life-sustaining treatment?

As mortal human beings, we live our lives knowing that we will die. To live well we should both cherish this precious gift of life and accept the inevitability of death. Christian faith gives us reason to cherish life, as a gift from God, and also gives reason to accept death, when it comes, with hope in God. It is important to acknowledge that our earthly life will come to an end and to prepare for this as well as we can. As death approaches, we need to be able to accept this reality and not seek futile treatment. Many people are anxious that they will not be allowed to die naturally and that they will be subjected to unwanted and unnecessary treatment. This is called over-treatment.

3.3 Which is worse, under-treatment or over-treatment?

Some people are more concerned about the danger of under-treatment, particularly of older people, fearing that they may be neglected or deprived of nutrition or hydration. They are rightly concerned with cherishing life. Others are more concerned about the danger of over-treatment, and the potential of modern medicine to make the dying process needlessly burdensome. They are rightly concerned with helping people to achieve a good death. We must acknowledge both of these concerns and recognise that people wish to influence how they are treated. If we focus on only one of these dangers we may fall into the opposite danger without being aware of it.

3.4 How does the Mental Capacity Act seek to address these concerns about under-treatment or over-treatment?

The Mental Capacity Act seeks to address concerns about over-treatment by including someone's wishes and feelings as part of what is in his or her best interests, and by encouraging people to plan ahead for a time when they lack capacity by naming a health and welfare attorney or by making an advance decision. These are ways in which the possibility of over-treatment can be anticipated and avoided.

To help avoid the problem of under-treatment, the Mental Capacity Act puts in place various safeguards: advance decisions must be valid and applicable; attorneys can be challenged; there is a new crime of death by neglect. For people with no one to speak for them, the Mental Capacity Act requires that independent advocates be appointed. These can challenge doctors not to neglect treatment which would be in the best interests of the patient. The Act requires that decisions about life-sustaining treatment must not be motivated by a desire to bring about the person's death (Mental Capacity Act s.4(5)) and this applies to attorneys as well as professionals.

3.5 Does the Mental Capacity Act change the law on so-called 'mercy killing' (euthanasia) or assisted suicide?

The Mental Capacity Act declares that 'nothing in this Act is to be taken to affect the law relating to murder or manslaughter or…assisting suicide' (s.62). Doing anything to cause death, even at the request of the patient and as an "act of mercy", remains murder in English law, and assisting a patient to commit suicide also remains a serious criminal offence. The Act unfortunately retains a feature of recent English law which has put the law in tension or even conflict with sound morality, namely, the law's acceptance of certain decisions to bring about death - one's own or someone else - by omission or withdrawal of life-sustaining treatment or of food or water in circumstances where, although death is not imminent, the decision-maker considers that continued life is not worthwhile. It is to be hoped that the interpretation of the Act will not widen the law's breach with the true moral principles which exclude homicide and suicide even by omission, and that all involved in healthcare will be permitted to make their decisions according to those principles. The Act's insistence that decisions about whether life-sustaining treatment is in someone's best interests must not be motivated by a desire to bring about death (s.4(5)) must be interpreted as excluding all intent to shorten life, whether by act or omission. Carers, healthcare workers and others who are in a position of power need to remain clear that it is never legitimate to give or omit treatment in order to bring about death.

3.6 What does the Mental Capacity Act say about advance decisions ('living wills')?

The Mental Capacity Act enables people to make a decision in advance to refuse treatment, if they should lack capacity to do so in the future. This is commonly known as a 'living will', but it is not a will in the ordinary sense of the word. Advance decisions have a different format and different rules apply to them from the rules that apply to a will. For example, someone can change their mind about an advance decision without having to write anything down - the Act makes clear that a simple word or even a change of behaviour is enough to make an advance decision invalid. But it is better to put any change of mind in writing.

If an advance decision concerns treatment that is necessary to sustain life, it must be in writing, signed and witnessed. It must also include the statement that the decision stands 'even if life is at risk' which must also be in writing, signed and witnessed. The Act also sets out two important safeguards of validity and applicability for advance decisions to refuse life-sustaining treatment. If the decision is not valid (signed, witnessed and made by someone who understands the consequences of what he or she is signing) or if it is not applicable to the circumstances, then it does not bind the healthcare team. On the other hand, if there is a valid and applicable advance refusal then treatment cannot legally be given, whether or not it is in the patient's best interests.

4. Choices about my future health and treatment

4.1 Can I in good conscience appoint a lasting power of attorney?

Yes. If you wish to appoint someone to make decisions on your behalf you should choose someone who knows you well and whom you trust to act wisely, morally and in your best interests. You should talk to him or her and discuss what it might involve.

4.2 Can I in good conscience make an advance decision?

Yes. There may be good reasons to decide against having a specific medical treatment in particular circumstances, and it is possible to state this in advance. When death is approaching, it is often useful to discuss different treatment or care possibilities with a doctor and to make a care plan. This might helpfully include an advance decision.

It is, however, difficult to predict what choices one might want to make in the absence of a diagnosis of a specific serious illness or degenerative condition. Therefore, it is generally inadvisable to make an advance decision to refuse treatment unless you are already ill or have a diagnosis in which serious illness or disability is predictable.

An advance decision to refuse treatment, if it were valid and applicable, could prevent a doctor from giving treatment which would have been in your best interests. This is therefore something to consider very carefully, and should only be done in consultation with your GP, hospital doctor or nurse. Advice about making an advance decision is included at the end of this booklet.

Not everything allowed by the Act is morally the right thing to do. For example, refusal of food and fluids is morally unacceptable (when death is not imminent) unless they can neither provide nourishment nor alleviate suffering, or cannot be taken without really significant physical discomfort.

4.3 If I make an advance decision, when will it be implemented?

An advance decision is only implemented when you lack capacity to consent to the treatment in question and when it is applicable to your situation.

4.4 Can I change my mind?

Yes. You can change your mind at any time. You do not have to put the change in writing. If you make your change of mind clear either verbally or by your behaviour, then the advance decision is no longer valid. Nevertheless, it is better to put any change of mind in writing in case it is forgotten or disputed. Furthermore, you may not get a chance to express your change of mind and this is something to remember when making an advance decision. You should be careful that your decision is one that you can reasonably expect to remain happy with.

4.5 Can I make a choice about what treatment I would like?

Yes and no. You can make a request for treatment, and doctors must consider your wishes, but in general you cannot demand a particular treatment. A healthcare professional is not obliged to provide treatment which is not in the best interests of the patient. However, in deciding what is in the best interests of the patient, the health professionals must take wishes and feelings into consideration.

Furthermore, patients can demand entirely appropriate treatment that they consider is in their best interests. If this were refused in an attempt to bring about the death of the patient it would be a serious crime. Speaking in the *Leslie Burke* case, Lord Phillips, said, 'where a competent patient indicates his or her wish to be kept alive by the provision of artificial nutrition and hydration (ANH) any doctor who deliberately brings that patient's life to an end by discontinuing the supply of ANH will not merely be in breach of duty but guilty of murder.' (*[2006] QB 273 Page 302)*

4.6 Can doctors and nurses make decisions about my treatment without asking me?

In ordinary circumstances doctors and nurses should not make decisions about your treatment without asking you. They should make all practicable efforts to support you in making your own decisions. If you are not able to make a rational decision but are still conscious then they should seek to involve you in the decision. The Mental Capacity Act aims to protect the right of people to make decisions for themselves.

4.7 If I cannot make a choice, who will decide for me?

If you cannot make a decision then a doctor or whoever is caring for you will make a decision on your behalf. This must be done in your best interests and considering your past and present wishes and feelings. The Mental Capacity Act obliges healthcare professionals to take reasonable steps to consult anyone you have named, your health and welfare attorney if you have appointed one, and your carers and those close to you. If there are no friends or relatives who can be contacted and serious decisions have to be made, for example about withdrawal of treatment or about transfer to a care home, then the relevant local authority or NHS organisation is responsible for instructing an independent mental capacity advocate to represent you.

Doctors have a general obligation to provide treatment in your best interests. If a proposed treatment would be futile and death imminent, then in all likelihood it is not in your best interests to receive that treatment. If it is practical to do so, medical professionals should involve named people, attorneys, carers, relatives and friends in the decision not to intervene.

An advantage of a written statement of wishes and feelings, as discussed at the end of this booklet, is that it can help guide those who have to make decisions about your care and can name people who should be consulted.

4.8 Do I have a moral obligation to accept treatment?

Not necessarily. You have a moral obligation to accept some treatments, for you have a duty to care for your health for your own sake and for the sake of others who may rely on you. However, some treatments impose heavy burdens or offer little benefit, and as death approaches, further treatment may be futile.

4.9 Do I always have to have life-prolonging treatment?

No. How you spend your time on earth is more important than the length of your life. Though you have a duty to care for your health, you do not have a duty to prolong your life at all costs. As death approaches a treatment which may briefly prolong your life could impose suffering such that you consider the treatment is excessively burdensome.

4.10 Is there a difference between deciding not to have a treatment and stopping a treatment which has been started?

There is at least a psychological difference between deciding not to have a treatment and deciding to stop a treatment which has been started. It may feel more difficult emotionally to stop something than deciding not to start it in the first place. However, we cannot always know whether a treatment will work until we have tried it. We should not discourage people from starting treatment simply to avoid anxiety about discontinuing it.

4.11 Can I morally allow illness to take its natural course, even if this means I will die?

Yes under some circumstances. There are two things that need to be kept in mind here: cherishing life and accepting death. Cherishing life entails that death should not be the aim of our action or of our inaction.

We should not try to bring about death. On the other hand, accepting death from God entails that we should not flee from the inevitable by seeking unreasonable treatment.

4.12 What does the Catechism say about withdrawal of treatment?

Catholic teaching about withdrawal of treatment is set out briefly in the *Catechism of the Catholic Church* (paragraph 2278):

> 'Discontinuing medical procedures that are burdensome, dangerous, extraordinary, or disproportionate to their expected outcome can be legitimate: it is the refusal of 'over-zealous' treatment. Here one does not will to cause death; one's inability to impede it is merely accepted. The decision should be made by the patient if he is competent and able or, if not, by those legally entitled to act for the patient, whose reasonable will and legitimate interests must always be respected.'

4.13 Can every sort of treatment be withdrawn?

The Code of Practice recognises that there are some measures, sometimes called basic or essential care, that are necessary to keep a patient comfortable and these should rarely if ever be withdrawn. Neither an advance decision nor an attorney can refuse the provision of warmth, shelter, or actions to keep a person clean. If a person can swallow and digest safely then he or she should always be offered food and water by mouth. Health professionals should continue to provide such care in the best interests of the person lacking capacity. Many patients with serious mental incapacity may not have the ability or strength to ask for or accept a drink or may not be able to swallow properly. The law requires that these patients are not neglected and that they do not suffer needlessly as a result of hunger or dehydration.

According to the Code of Practice 'artificial nutrition and hydration' should be considered as a medical treatment, and therefore as something that can be withheld or withdrawn. Artificial nutrition and hydration involves using tubes to provide nutrition and fluids to someone who cannot take them by mouth. It bypasses the natural mechanisms of eating and drinking and requires clinical monitoring. Nevertheless, the administration of water and food, even when provided by artificial means, always represents a natural means of preserving life, and is not itself a medical act. For this reason it is better to talk of assisted nutrition and hydration. In English law the administration of nutrition and hydration by tube is regarded as a form of medical treatment, but from an ethical standpoint it should be regarded as basic care which should not be withdrawn unless it can neither provide nourishment nor alleviate suffering, or cannot be taken without really significant physical discomfort.

A decision to withhold or withdraw tube feeding must be made on the basis of the best interests of the individual and must be made with the right intention. There are certainly cases where withdrawal of artificially delivered food and fluids would be harmful, for example where there is a good chance of recovery or where the death of a person, who is seriously ill or disabled, is not imminent. In such cases withholding or withdrawing tube feeding would cause dehydration and could bring about death as a consequence. This would clearly be against the person's best interests. On the other hand, in the last few days of life it may not be in someone's best interests to give food and fluids by tube if, for example, food and fluids can no longer be absorbed or excreted by the body, or if withdrawal of food and fluid would not hasten death and the tube causes significant discomfort. In addition, any decision to withdraw treatment or care must also be made with the right intention. It must never be done with the aim of hastening that person's death.

4.14 What did Pope John Paul II say about using assisted means to provide food and fluids?

Pope John Paul II, writing about people who are not dying but who are in a 'vegetative state', stated that it is obligatory to provide nutrition and hydration even if this must be done by artificial means:

> 'I should like particularly, to underline how the administration of water and food, even when provided by artificial means, always represents a natural means of preserving life, not a medical act. Its use, furthermore, should be considered, in principle, ordinary and proportionate, and as such morally obligatory, insofar as and until it is seen to have attained its proper finality, which in the present case consists in providing nourishment to the patient and alleviation of his suffering. The obligation to provide "the normal care due to the sick" in such cases includes, in fact, the use of nutrition and hydration.'

The Congregation for the Doctrine of the Faith has reiterated this teaching in its '*Responses to Certain Questions of the United States Conference of Catholic Bishops concerning Artificial Nutrition and Hydration, with Commentary*' (1st August 2007).

4.15 What am I entitled to expect from the people caring for me?

You are entitled to expect that people will act in your best interests, will give the nursing care and comfort that you need, will consider your wishes, and will not give medical treatment that you have refused in an advance decision document. You can help health and social care professionals by drawing up a *written statement of wishes and feelings expressing* your values and by having accessible the contact details of someone they can consult about your wishes and concerns. Written statements and named persons to consult will give the professionals information to help them care for you, but will not bind them in a way that might prejudice your future care.

5. Issues for health and social care professionals

5.1 What are the implications for me?

As a social or healthcare professional, you have a duty to be familiar with the Mental Capacity Act and with the Code of Practice and to apply these consistently in a way that will respect the person in your care and not bring him or her to harm.

The principles of the Act, correctly understood, set out your key moral responsibilities: to enable individuals to make reasonable decisions regarding their own healthcare and, where this is not possible, to act in their best interests. This will include making reasonable efforts to consult those named by the individual or failing that those close to him or her when making significant decisions.

Health and social care professionals need to be aware of the provisions of the Act that relate to the assessment of a person's capacity.

5.2 How do I identify what is in someone's best interests?

The Mental Capacity Act gives a list of factors to be taken into account when assessing best interests (Mental Capacity Act s.4(1)-(7)). The first rule is that best interests must not be determined purely on the basis of age, medical condition or behaviour. Best interests decisions are not to be made on the basis of prejudice about what it is to live with a particular condition. The Mental Capacity Act also requires that decision makers take into account the likelihood of recovery of capacity and the known wishes of the person. Nevertheless, while wishes and feelings must be taken into account, the Code of Practice makes clear that these may not be the deciding factor and that what matters is what is truly in someone's best interests in a particular situation.

In English law, "best interests" has an objective meaning which is not reducible to the wishes and feelings someone happens to have. The Mental Capacity Act does not state explicitly but presupposes that the health, life and wellbeing of the patient are in his or her interest. For example, the Mental Capacity Act presupposes the duties of a doctor (as outlined by the General Medical Council) to 'show respect for human life', to 'make the care of your patient your first concern' and to 'protect and promote the health of patients'.

Where the determination relates to life-sustaining treatment, the Mental Capacity Act lays down that the best interests decision must not be 'motivated by a desire to bring about the patient's death' (Mental Capacity Act s.4(5)). In some other parts of English law, 'being motivated by a desire' includes not only desiring something for its own sake (as an end or ultimate motive) but also purposing, intending or choosing something as a means, and that is how s.4(5) should be interpreted. A decision to withdraw treatment in order to bring about someone's death is not moral, and should be taken to be excluded by the Act, even when the decision's ultimate motive is not that person's death for its own sake but death is being willed as a means of, for example, relieving hardship or expense. On the other hand, where treatment is withdrawn because it is futile or unduly burdensome, this may be in the best interests of someone even where it is foreseen that it may also hasten that person's death. Best interests relate to the benefits and burdens of treatment and should never reflect a judgement that the patient's life is not worth living.

5.3 If I am concerned about a patient's treatment or care, what can I do?

Usually the first thing is to establish the facts as fully as possible by asking questions. It may be that there are aspects of the case of which you are unaware. It may be that by raising questions you can help colleagues, or relatives, to articulate what they hope for from treatment or non-treatment. There may be other concerns at work besides the best interests of the patient, or there may be a distorted view of what would be in his or her best interests. These issues can be addressed once they are in the open.

Talking things through is the first step to achieving good practice. The law is of limited value once communication has broken down. The other prerequisite of good practice is a positive ethos of care within the healthcare setting. Particular healthcare decisions depend on many details and cannot be reduced to a set of rules. Without a supportive environment, decisions may be made insensitively and people may be in danger of under-treatment or over-treatment. Good care may be easier to achieve in the relatively sheltered environment of a hospice, small unit, or care home, but it is important to encourage good practice as far as possible in all healthcare settings.

5.4 If I am concerned that an advance decision is not in the best interests of the patient, what should I do?

In law, an advance refusal may be valid even where it could be considered unwise. Thus, if a refusal relates to treatment which would be in the best interests of the patient, great care must be taken to determine if the refusal is actually valid and is applicable to the circumstances. Where a health professional is not satisfied that a valid and applicable advance decision exists, it would be considered lawful to treat that patient in their best interests. In cases where there is reasonable doubt about the validity or applicability of the advance decision, and especially in emergency situations, the professional is not liable if he or she treats a patient according to best interests, and indeed it would be their professional responsibility to do so until the nature of the illness and the applicability of the advance decision had been confirmed.

For instance, where a person has made an advance decisions many years previously, and at a time when they were not suffering from any illness or disease, then there may well be reasonable doubt as to whether it is in fact valid and applicable to the specific situation.

On the other hand, where there is an advance decision to refuse treatment and this is clearly valid and applicable to the situation, it is illegal to give treatment. This is similar to the situation of someone who is conscious and able to make the decision and who refuses treatment. The law forbids the doctor from imposing treatment in these circumstances, even if the treatment would save the person's life. This is hard for a conscientious doctor who is committed to the best interests of those in his or her care. Nevertheless, if there is a valid and applicable refusal of treatment, and if providing the treatment would have sufficiently grave legal consequences for the doctor, then he is not guilty of neglect for any harm that follows from his not providing it. This is because the law in effect removes this aspect of the person's care from the doctor's professional responsibility.

5.5 If I am concerned that an advance decision may be suicidal what should I do?

The Mental Capacity Act states that any act done, or decision made, under the Act must be done, or made, in the best interests of the patient (Mental Capacity Act s.1(5)) and that judgements regarding best interests should not be motivated by a desire to bring about the death of the patient (Mental Capacity Act s.4(5)). It explicitly states that it does not change the prohibition on assisted suicide and euthanasia (Mental Capacity Act s.62).

It is important to realise that a refusal of life-sustaining treatment is not necessarily suicidal. Someone may refuse treatment because it is burdensome or risky or because they are not convinced of the benefits. A refusal will only be suicidal if someone refuses medical treatment with the specific aim of ending his or her life by these means. The aim or intention of the person who refuses treatment will not always be evident to others. In general, it cannot simply be 'read off' or deduced from the advance decision document itself, because the reason for the refusal will not usually be recorded. A healthcare worker should give a patient the benefit of the doubt and should not assume that a refusal reflects a suicidal intention.

In the case of a suicide note which included a refusal of treatment, it is doubtful that this would fulfil the legal requirements for a valid and applicable advance decision. A valid advance decision to withhold life-sustaining treatment must be witnessed and must use the right form of words (Mental Capacity Act s.25(5), s.25(6)). What is more, even if these requirements were fulfilled, the Code of Practice states that, if someone is clearly suicidal, this raises questions about that person's capacity to make an advance decision at the time he or she made it (Code of Practice 9.9). As stated above, in cases of reasonable doubt, and especially in emergency situations, the professional is not liable if he or she treats a patient according to best interests.

In rare cases where a refusal is clearly suicidal and is definitely valid and applicable we need to understand the refusal on two levels: the refusal itself, and possible cooperation with this refusal.

If a refusal of treatment is intended to bring about death then it is suicidal. Such a refusal is a self-destructive act that also harms society and fails to acknowledge life as a gift from God. Even if this refusal is legally permitted, it is not something that should be done.

A second and related question is to what extent we can morally 'co-operate' with someone's suicidal refusal. For example, should we carry out the person's wishes by withdrawing a feeding tube or by ordering others to withdraw it? The Church teaches that 'voluntary cooperation in suicide is contrary to the moral law' (*Catechism of the Catholic Church* 2282). In the rare case where a decision to refuse treatment is made clearly and explicitly for suicidal reasons then doctors and healthcare workers should not do anything to imply approval of the decision. They should make clear that morally they cannot implement an overtly suicidal request to withdraw treatment. In some cases, this may necessitate the professional's withdrawal from the patient's care. This is allowed for by the Code of Practice; see question 5.9 in this Guide: *Is there a conscientious objection clause in the Mental Capacity Act?* A short explanation of the Church's teaching on cooperation can be found in the Appendix to this Guide, which reproduces an extract from the Bishops' Conference teaching document *Cherishing Life*.

5.6 Must I respect an advance refusal of artificial nutrition and hydration?

The Mental Capacity Act allows people to refuse 'artificial nutrition and hydration' in specified circumstances. If this refusal is a valid and applicable advance refusal then it is illegal to provide nutrition or hydration by artificial means. This is so even where withholding nutrition and hydration will lead to the person's death. Nevertheless, the Code of Practice also says that 'an advance decision cannot refuse actions that are needed to keep a person comfortable' (Code of Practice 9.28). Fluids should always be given if they are necessary to alleviate a person's distress.

Artificially provided nutrition and hydration should not be put in the same category as medical treatment. Nutrition and hydration, however they are provided, should be classed as basic care that should, in principle, always be provided. Only when someone is close to death can it sometimes be justifiable to withdraw nutrition and hydration (see also section 4.13 p25-26). If someone is ill but not near death then, even if a refusal of artificial nutrition and hydration is not intended to bring about death, it will have this effect. A refusal of nutrition and hydration would prevent carers from providing basic care and so the law ought to have given doctors and healthcare workers the authority to override such a refusal. However, the Code of Practice explicitly considers artificial nutrition and hydration as medical treatment that can be refused.

In this situation healthcare professionals should strive to do everything they can in the best interests of the their patient but, having tried their best, the law may not give them the power to provide the care they would wish. Trying their best should include assessing very carefully whether or not the advance refusal is specific, valid and applicable to the immediate situation, and also whether providing fluids might be needed to keep the person comfortable. If healthcare professionals are in any reasonable doubt about whether the advance refusal is in fact valid and applicable to the immediate decision they face, they must continue to provide assisted nutrition and hydration where they believe doing so to be in the best interests of the patient as long as the patient remains their responsibility. In cases of dispute they should apply to the Court of Protection for an adjudication. If all other remedies fail then they should not formally cooperate with the withdrawal of this aspect of care (if this withdrawal is clearly against the best interests of the patient). They may have to withdraw from the care of the patient altogether.

5.7 Who should speak on behalf of the patient?

If someone is unable to communicate, even with assistance, the Mental Capacity Act requires health and social care professionals to take reasonable steps to consult any named persons, and relatives or carers, when making care decisions in the best interests of someone who lacks capacity. The 'next of kin' has never, in fact, enjoyed in English law any privileged legal status in regard to healthcare decisions. The term is merely useful shorthand for someone close to the person, whom the person would want informed and involved in any decision making.

The presence of a *written statement of wishes and feelings* specifying a named person or persons to be consulted could help resolve what is often a cause of tension between friends or relatives. It can happen that relatives do not approve of those who are caring for the patient, or a member of a Religious Congregation may want decisions taken by his or her named community representative, rather than by a relative. Similarly, someone may want to make sure that a spouse or a close friend is not excluded by the family.

The Lasting Power of Attorney empowers an attorney to make decisions in the best interests of the person who cannot make decisions for himself or herself. An unnamed office holder (for example, the superior of a religious order) cannot be designated as an attorney, as the attorney must be a named individual. For this reason a written statement of wishes and feelings may be especially useful for a member of a religious community.

A Lasting Power of Attorney for Health and Welfare, which authorises the attorney to make decisions about withholding or withdrawing treatment, confers a serious responsibility which must be exercised with care in the person's best interests. If the person's death is not imminent then the decision of an attorney to withdraw nutrition and hydration is not in the best interests of that person. The decisions of an attorney must never be 'motivated by a desire to bring about the person's death'. (Mental Capacity Act s.4(5)) or involve the intention to bring about death.

5.8 What happens if I disagree with an attorney?

Health and social care professionals must respect the power that is given to an attorney giving them the benefit of the doubt as far as is reasonable. The attorney has the power to refuse consent to treatment if he or she considers that it is not in the best interests of the patient. Suggestions of treatment from the attorney, while not binding, must be considered seriously.

If a member of the healthcare team disagrees with an attorney about withdrawing treatment the first step should be to discuss with the attorney the best interests of the patient. If agreement cannot be reached, and the professional has strong grounds to suspect the motives or the intentions of the attorney, then the Office of the Public Guardian can be asked to intervene. If there is no question of unlawful motives or intentions, but the professional thinks that the course of action is not in the best interests of the patient (for example, where there is a reasonable chance that a patient may recover capacity if given treatment, but an attorney is refusing permission), then the healthcare professional can appeal to the Court of Protection. If a case goes to court healthcare professionals can treat the patient in what they regard as their best interests in the interim without fear of liability. This series of steps may require considerable determination on the part of a professional to safeguard the best interests of the patient.

5.9 Is there a conscientious objection clause in the Mental Capacity Act?

The Mental Capacity Act 2005 does not contain an explicit section on conscientious objection. Nevertheless the issue is addressed in the Code of Practice (9.61-9.63). The Code states that there is a general legal framework that already protects the consciences of professionals. This framework is summarised by two points:

- Health and social care professionals do not have to do something that goes against their beliefs.
- Health and social care professionals must not simply abandon patients or cause their care to suffer.

According to the Code, if a patient who lacks capacity has made a valid and applicable advance decision to refuse treatment, which a health professional cannot, for reasons of conscience, comply with, then the patient should be transferred to the care of someone else and the professional should let their viewpoint be known immediately to their line manager or deputy who will need to take responsibility for the patient's subsequent management. Concerns which lead to this action should be documented by the professional whose conscience dictates an inability to carry on the management of the patient.

In practice the difficult issues are most likely to arise where there is a disagreement between healthcare professionals, or between a healthcare professional and a relative, about whether an advance decision is valid and applicable, or about what is in the best interests of the patient. In many cases, familiarity with the Mental Capacity Act and the Code of Practice will help a healthcare professional in arguing against actions that are not in the best interests of a patient.

If you think a management plan is unethical, then you should speak with, and listen to, colleagues and relatives. You will need to satisfy yourself, in line with your duty of care that the person was aware or that the attorney or those close to the person are aware of the consequences of withdrawing treatment, for example, of the effects of withdrawing artificially delivered food and fluid. If you remain sure that the planned course of action would not be in the best interests of the patient, and you cannot find support from others in this view, then you must not formally cooperate with this action. This may mean you have to withdraw from the care of that patient.

If the situation is one that involves not formal but material cooperation, you should carefully weigh up the alternatives in the light of your moral obligations, giving consideration to the danger of misleading others, the disadvantages to the patient's care, and the personal cost. The moral assessment of material cooperation is complex and it is impossible to give simple hard and fast rules as there are many factors to be taken into account in a particular situation. A short explanation of the Church's teaching on cooperation can be found in the Appendix to this Guide, which reproduces an extract from the Bishops' Conference teaching document *Cherishing Life*.

6. How do I find out more?

6.1 Finding out more about the Mental Capacity Act

There are short guides to help you which can be obtained from:
http://www.justice.gov.uk/guidance/mca-info-booklets.htm

The Mental Capacity Act is accompanied by a Code of Practice that explains the details of how it will be implemented and what your legal responsibilities are. All health and social care employers should have a copy of this and it will help you to understand your legal situation. A free copy can be downloaded from the Ministry of Justice website at:
http://www.justice.gov.uk/guidance/mca-code-of-practice.htm

The Act makes further provision through the Court of Protection for situations where someone lacks capacity to appoint an attorney, or has not done so you can find more information about these provisions at: *www.guardianship.gov.uk*

6.2 Finding out more about planning for a time when I may not be able to make decisions for myself

One of the short guides mentioned above is entitled 'Planning ahead - a guide for people who wish to prepare for possible future incapacity'. This is one place to start.

Just as important as written guidance is talking to those who will be involved with your care or with making decisions that will affect you. This means first and foremost those you live with or those immediately involved in your care. They will be faced with making decisions in your best interests when you cannot make decisions for yourself. The guidance on *written statement of wishes and feelings* given below can help raise questions to discuss. Before taking the step of making an advance decision or granting a lasting power of attorney you should talk to a priest and also a family doctor or a consultant about the possible treatment and care decisions that might need to be considered in your case. In the case of a lasting power of attorney you should also consider seeking legal advice.

6.3 Finding out more about my responsibilities as a family member, a carer, or a health or social care professional

The Ministry of Justice has produced booklets for legal practitioners, for social care professionals, for healthcare professionals and for family and friends. A number of people will be under a formal duty to have regard to the Code of Practice: professionals and paid carers, people acting as attorneys and deputies appointed by the Court of Protection.

Copies of the Government booklets and help and guidance about the Act and the Code of Practice for family, friends and unpaid carers is available from: *http://www.justice.gov.uk/guidance/mca-info-booklets.htm*

In addition to the Code, and the booklets brought out by the Department of Health and the Ministry of Justice, many professional bodies will provide guidance to their members. Professionals will also need to be attentive to the guidance of regulatory bodies such as the General Medical Council.

6.4 Finding out more about the teaching of the Catholic Church on these issues

It is important to stress that none of the guidance given by the Mental Capacity Act or the Code of Practice is a substitute for making your own conscientious judgement on the case at hand. For Catholics, this judgement must be informed by, and in accordance with, the Church's teaching in these difficult areas.

Cherishing Life is a teaching document from the Catholic Bishops of England and Wales on life issues and it aims to inform conscience and encourage us all to contribute further to public debate, as each of us has an important role to play in influencing legislation and shaping values in today's society. It is available to buy as a book and also available online at: *www.catholic-ew.org.uk/cherishinglife/contents.htm*

The Linacre Centre for Healthcare Ethics (*www.linacre.org*) exists to help Catholics and others to explore the Church's position on bioethical issues. It has a wide range of publications and materials on its website and can also be contacted directly for advice on ethical issues.

The Guild of Catholic Doctors (*www.catholicdoctors.org.uk*) provides support to healthcare professionals especially in matters of conscience and offers informed opinion about the implications of developments in medicine and social policy.

Catholics in Healthcare (*www.catholicsinhealthcare.org.uk*) is a new and developing web-based resource designed to help Catholics working in health and social care fields in England and Wales to network with others, access resources and support, and live out their vocation as skilled, effective and committed care workers.

The Pontifical Council for Health Pastoral Care has published a number of useful documents including the *Charter for Healthcare Workers* (1995), see: *www.healthpastoral.org*

Pope John Paul II wrote extensively on ethical issues in medicine. His most important work in this area is *Evangelium Vitae* (1995). It is available to buy as a book and also available online at:
www.vatican.va/edocs/ENG0141/_INDEX.HTM

The *Catechism of the Catholic Church* is a rich source of guidance not only on matters of faith but also on ethical issues, especially in Part Three: Life in Christ. The Catechism is available to buy as a book and is also online at:
http://www.vatican.va/archive/ccc/

The Congregation for the Doctrine of the Faith *Responses to Certain Questions of the United States Conference of Catholic Bishops concerning Artificial Nutrition and Hydration, with Commentary* (1st August 2007) is available online at:
www.vatican.va/roman_curia/congregations/cfaith/doc_doc_index.htm

7. Advice on writing statements of wishes and feelings and making advance decisions

7.1 Statements of wishes and feelings

The Mental Capacity Act s.4(6(a)), s.4(7(a)) and Code of Practice (5.34, 5.37, 5.42-5.44) require professionals who care for people who cannot make decisions for themselves to take into account any statement of wishes and feelings those people have made. There is no requirement as to the form of such a statement, or that it be in writing. Expressions of wishes that are made verbally in conversation with health professionals and possibly recorded in a person's health record or as part of any agreed care plan have equal weight.

Some things that could be included in a statement of wishes and feelings are the names and contact details of people who you would want to be consulted if you could not make decisions for yourself.

If you are a Catholic then you should state somewhere that you wish a priest to be contacted, and to visit you if you become ill. The sacrament of the sick is not only for people who are dying but for those who are seriously ill and who need strength and consolation from God (See James 5:14-16).

You should say that you regard food and fluids as basic care, even when delivered by a tube. If you are anxious about the possibility of being neglected, then say so. If you are worried about receiving a particular treatment you do not want, then say so. A doctor will give you treatment in an emergency but he or she will have to take your wishes into account.

A statement of wishes and feeling might also concern where you wish to be looked after or how you wish money to be spent.

These are just suggestions as to things you might include in a statement. This booklet does not give an example in case people think that they need to say things in a specific way. If it is a clear statement of what is important to you in your own words then it will be useful to people who look after you.

7.2 Advance decisions to refuse treatment

The guidance given in this section is not recommending that people should make an advance decision to refuse treatment, and is certainly not suggesting any particular decision you should make. It gives examples of the kind of advance decisions some people might make. This shows what you need to think about if you wish to make an advance decision.

The Mental Capacity Act has formalised the process for individuals to make a decision to refuse treatment, if they should lack capacity to do so in the future. This is known as an advance decision. It only comes into effect if the person is unable to make their own decision at the time and if it is both valid and applicable to the situation.

'Valid' means that the decision was made at a time when the person was over 18 and had capacity to do so. It does not need to be written down unless it concerns refusal of life-sustaining treatment. However, writing down any such decision, and discussing it with relevant family or professionals can help to avoid later confusion or concern about its validity. If the person has subsequently appointed a health and welfare LPA to make decisions regarding this treatment, then the previous advance decision is no longer valid.

'Applicable' means that the advance decision clearly applies to the circumstances and treatment now in question. If there have been changes in the person's circumstances such that there is reasonable doubt that the person may not have made such an advance decision, it may not be applicable.

Making an advance decision

Many people, particularly those who live with illness or disability develop views about the types of treatment they wish to have or to refuse. It is helpful to discuss these with family, carers and professionals particularly if there is a possibility that the ability to communicate or capacity to make decisions may be lost and to record them in writing so that they are borne in mind for the future. Although it can feel difficult to contemplate deteriorating health, it is advisable to have such discussions while it is still possible, in the knowledge that your treatment and care can be planned in a way that you agree with.

An advance decision can only specify treatments that you would not wish to have. It is important to understand the implications of such a refusal, both in terms of subsequent health and whether the treatment might be considered life-sustaining. It is wise therefore to consider discussing these with a doctor or other health professional who knows about the condition.

The following are **examples of situations** where people may wish to refuse treatment. They are not exhaustive and should only be considered as a guide to the types of treatment that individuals sometimes wish to avoid. They are given to show how advance decisions are specific to a person and to his or her circumstances.

In end stage lung disease or end stage heart failure people may reach a stage where they do not wish to be re-admitted to hospital for treatment of the next infection or flare up, particularly if treatment is becoming ineffective. In this situation, they may make an advance decision to refuse such treatment and remain at home with support from their GP and other health professionals.

Another example might be a decision about life-sustaining treatment. To be valid and applicable such an advance decision cannot be a blanket statement, for example to refuse 'all life-sustaining treatment'. It must specify which particular treatments are being refused and in what circumstances this refusal applies. It would be desirable also to add the reason for this decision which of course should never be in order to bring about death.

Dementia, Multiple Sclerosis or Parkinson's Disease, are examples of illnesses where capacity may be lost in the later stages. A person may wish to refuse in advance specific treatment they think is excessive when life expectancy is short, such as artificial ventilation or intravenous antibiotics for infection. Or in the final stage of a progressive illness a person may refuse to have a feeding tube put into the stomach (what is sometimes called a 'PEG' tube) if maintaining nutrition in this way would cause significant physical discomfort and is not going to prevent their imminent death. Or in the same circumstances they might consent to the insertion of such a tube but say that, if the tube becomes infected, which is usually associated with localised pain, then they would want it withdrawn and not replaced.

These kinds of refusals would not exclude treatments aimed at relieving symptoms (including subcutaneous fluids under the skin) and maintaining comfort and dignity - these are part of basic care which should never be withdrawn.

It is not possible to consider all eventualities but through discussion with people involved in their care, individuals may wish to specify treatment they want to avoid. If this is for particular reasons, then it helps to state your reasons.

If an advance decision concerns refusal of some life-sustaining treatment, then this must be put in writing, together with a statement that specifies the refusal 'even if my life is at risk'. The document must also be witnessed. It should be kept in a place where it can be accessed such as the GP, hospital or nursing home record, or in a known place at home.

If you are planning to make an advance decision to refuse treatment you should be clear about your motives: your intention should simply be to avoid treatment which you believe would be excessive, involve unwise risk or be futile. You should not refuse treatment in order to hasten your own death. The effect of an advance refusal may be that you will die sooner, but that should not be your aim. Furthermore, you should not refuse assisted nutrition and hydration unless it can neither provide nourishment nor alleviate suffering, or it cannot be taken without really significant physical discomfort.

Appendix - Moral Foundations: the Church's teaching on character and conscience

(The following paragraphs are extracts from the teaching document of the Bishops of England and Wales, Cherishing Life, published in 2004, paragraphs 41-47)

'Make a tree sound and its fruits will be sound; make a tree rotten and its fruits will be rotten' (Matthew 12:33). Good actions can only be sustained by a good and reliable character. Character is formed through the many everyday practices, actions and decisions which either draw a person closer to God, to others and to personal integrity, or lead towards alienation from self, others and God. Through good actions we grow in the virtues. For example, practical wisdom helps us make the right choice. A just disposition secures fairness in our relations with others. Temperateness or moderation builds a right attitude to the goods of the world. Courage overcomes fear so that we can act well in the face of danger. Through prayer, the sacraments, and loving action, the Christian grows in faith, hope and the love of God.

Growth in virtue involves a deepening sensitivity towards what is right and wrong. It begins with the determination to live rightly and the willingness to learn how to judge wisely. The ability to make considered judgements recognising the moral quality of an action is termed 'conscience'. The judgement of conscience should be a prayerful one, made in consultation with people we can trust, with the aim of conforming to the truth. It should be adequately informed about the moral principles that apply to the act as these determine the moral quality of the act, as well as the circumstances and the intended moral good. In this judgement, a person confirms and takes responsibility for his or her own actions. Conscience is, then, that personal core and sanctuary where an individual stands before God.

Moral maturity involves growing in wisdom and in grace within and with the help of a community so as to be able to make the right judgements in particular situations. Christians see this as part of conversion to Christ. It is a life-long task. Education of character and conscience is a gradual process in which the developmental stage of each person needs to be respected. It is first situated in the home, within the family and in the local Church community, including its schools. Here a process begins which continues insofar as each person takes increasing responsibility for his or her own learning. Continuing adult education is important in a world of rapid change and new moral questions; for instance, in the fields of medicine, technology, economics and politics.

Conscience may be clouded by cultural perspectives or by honest ignorance, but in such cases the judgement of conscience does not lose its value. If someone has sincerely tried to discover and to follow the truth, but has mistakenly done something wrong, then he or she will not be at fault. Everyone is bound to follow their own best judgements and to take responsibility for their actions. However, recklessness or an unwillingness to find out what is the right thing to do will not excuse a person from blame if his or her bad choices result in wrong actions. Ignorance is not always an excuse.

Many factors will influence a person's moral judgement: experience, family, culture, and faith community. Often an individual will be hampered in living truthfully because he or she lacks freedom in particular moral choices. The academic disciplines of psychology, the study of family systems, class analysis and economics can all help illuminate these limits to freedom in relation to the development of personality. Nevertheless, while the effects of trauma or dysfunctional family background cannot be overcome easily, with God's help there can be psychological and spiritual healing and growth.

While everyone should seek to avoid doing wrong, sometimes it is impossible to avoid co-operating in the wrongdoing of others. For example, a good citizen should pay tax to contribute to schools, hospitals and upholding law and order, but it is very likely that some of this money will be used in ways that some people would find unconscionable, for instance, in paying for weapons of mass destruction. Catholic moral theology distinguishes two kinds of cooperation, formal and material. Formal cooperation means both actively helping and sharing the evil aims of the other person. This is something a conscientious person should never do. Material cooperation means helping someone accomplish something but without sharing that person's aims. Such cooperation can still be morally wrong, but at times it may be morally justified, for example, when one cannot opt out without jeopardising even more fundamental human goods than the evil tolerated. To return to our example, it is still right in principle to pay taxes even when we know that some of the money will be misspent.

The moral assessment of material cooperation is complex. It requires practical wisdom to take full account of the various factors involved and reach a judgement of conscience: Are there alternatives available? How urgent is it to act? What goods and what harms are at stake? How do each of these goods and harms relate to the action? Is there a reasonable likelihood of misleading others and thereby 'giving scandal'? What are the precise circumstances of the situation? How does this action conform with the individual's particular role, responsibilities and vocation? Consider the case of someone who works for a company that supplies medical instruments and who becomes aware that the company has recently started supplying abortion clinics. Having recognised this, one person may be called by God to object to such involvement, even at the risk losing this job, so as to bear prophetic witness to the evil that is being done. Someone else might recognise that abortion is wrong, but legitimately accept this level of cooperation in order faithfully to follow his or her vocation to support a family or for the sake of other worthwhile goals.

Glossary of terms

Advance Decision (or 'Living Will')	A decision to refuse specified treatment made in advance by a person who has **capacity** to do so. This decision will then apply at a future time when that person lacks **capacity** to consent to, or refuse, the specified treatment. Specific rules apply to advance decisions to refuse **life-sustaining treatment**. An advance decision is sometimes also known as a 'Living Will' but this term can be misleading and the Mental Capacity Act uses 'advance decision' instead.
Artificial Nutrition and Hydration (ANH)	Artificial nutrition and hydration (ANH) involves using tubes to provide nutrition and fluids to someone who cannot take them by mouth. It bypasses the natural mechanisms of eating and drinking and requires clinical monitoring. Nevertheless, the administration of water and food, even when provided by artificial means, always represents a natural means of preserving life, and is not itself a medical act. For this reason it is better to talk of assisted nutrition and hydration. In English law ANH is regarded as a form of medical treatment. However, the administration of nutrition and hydration should be regarded as basic care which should only be withdrawn if it can neither provide nourishment nor alleviate suffering, or cannot be taken without really significant physical discomfort.
Assisted Suicide	Helping a person to take his or her own life. Assisting suicide is a crime. Section 62 of the Mental Capacity Act states explicitly that assisted suicide remains a criminal offence.
Attorney	Someone appointed under either a **Lasting Power of Attorney** (LPA) or an **Enduring power of Attorney** (EPA), who has the legal right to make decisions within the scope of his or her authority in the **best interests** of the person (the donor) who made the power of attorney.
Basic Care	Care such as providing food and fluid, keeping a person comfortable and attending to his or her physical and other needs. In principle basic care should always to be provided, unless it is impractical or excessively burdensome to do so. Basic care is distinguished from medical treatment which may be withdrawn if it is not in the **best interests** of the patient.
Best Interests	Any decisions made about, or on behalf of a person who lacks **capacity** to make those specific decisions, must be in the person's best interests. The decision must focus on the best

	way to address the person's true needs, such as the need for life and health and the need for human relationship. Best interests relate to the reasonable hope of benefits without disproportionate burdens of treatment and should never reflect a judgement that the patient's life is not worth living. The Mental Capacity Act requires that someone's wishes and feelings be taken into account when assessing best interests. Nevertheless, both in law and in ethics 'best interests' should be given an objective meaning not reducible to wishes and feelings.
Capacity	The ability to make a decision about a particular matter at the time the decision needs to be made. The legal definition of a person who lacks capacity is set out in section 2 of the Mental Capacity Act.
Cherishing Life	A teaching document on Life issues published in 2004 by the Catholic Bishops' Conference of England and Wales.
Code of Practice	A statutory Code accompanying the Mental Capacity Act specifying in detail how key provisions of the Act are to be interpreted and applied in practice.
Court of Protection	The specialist Court for all issues relating to people who lack capacity to make specific decisions. The Court of Protection is established under section 45 of the Mental Capacity Act and cases can be referred to adjudicate disputes regarding sustaining treatment, **advance decisions** and also where decisions need to be made regarding children and young people.
Deputy	Someone appointed by the **Court of Protection** to make decisions in the **best interests** of a person who lacks **capacity** to make particular decisions.
Donor	A person who makes a **Lasting Power of Attorney**.
End of Life Decisions	A decision regarding the care and medical treatment of a person when that person is dying. The Catholic Church teaches that when death is imminent and inevitable it may be appropriate to withhold or withdraw medical treatment because it is judged to be unduly burdensome or futile. Such end of life decisions are not at all the same as **euthanasia** where the intention is to kill the person.
Enduring Power of Attorney (EPA)	A Power of Attorney created to deal with the donor's property and financial affairs. Existing EPAs will continue to operate under the Mental Capacity Act.

Euthanasia	So called 'mercy killing', where a person who is ill is intentionally killed in order to relieve his or her suffering. Euthanasia is a form of murder and remains a crime. The Mental Capacity Act states explicitly that the law against euthanasia remains unaffected by it (section 62).
Euthanasia by Omission	Where a person who is ill is deliberately deprived of treatment or care in order to bring about his or her death. The Mental Capacity Act states that best interests decisions must not be 'motivated by a desire to bring about the patient's death'. In some other parts of English law, 'being motivated by a desire' includes not only desiring something for its own sake (as an end or ultimate motive) but also purposing, intending or choosing something as a means, and that is how this provision of the Act should be interpreted. A decision to withdraw treatment in order to bring about someone's death is not moral, and should be taken to be excluded by this provision of the Act, even when the decision's ultimate motive is not that person's death for its own sake.
Formal Cooperation	Formal cooperation with wrongdoing is helping someone to do something wrong in such a way that one intends the object of the primary wrongdoer's activity. Helping in this context includes active participation in the action, as well as ordering, advising or praising the action, or not hindering the action when we could have done. It is never right to co-operate formally with wrongdoing. Formal cooperation is to be distinguished from **material cooperation**, which can sometimes be morally justified. (See definition of material cooperation below and also the further explanation in the Appendix)
Futile	A medical treatment may be described as futile when in the particular circumstances under consideration that treatment will not achieve its intended purpose. An example of futile treatment would be giving an antibiotic to a patient to treat an infection when the infection is known to be resistant to that treatment.
Independent Mental Capac -ity Advocate (IMCA)	Someone who provides support and representation for a person who lacks **capacity** to make specific decisions, where the person has no-one else to support him or her.
Incapacity	A person who lacks the **capacity** to make a particular decision.

Lasting Power of Attorney (LPA)	A Power of Attorney created under the Act to make decisions about the donor's personal welfare (including healthcare) and/or deal with the donor's property and affairs.
Life-sustaining Treatment	Treatment that, in the view of those providing healthcare, is necessary to keep a person alive and/or without which, he or she is likely to die.
Living Will	A short-hand term for an **Advance Decision**. The term 'living will' can be misleading and the Mental Capacity Act uses **advance decision** instead.
Material Cooperation	Material cooperation with wrongdoing is helping someone to do something wrong but without sharing that person's aims or intentions. Such cooperation can still be morally wrong, but at times it may be morally justified, for example, when one cannot opt out without jeopardising even more fundamental human goods than the evil tolerated. The moral assessment of material cooperation is complex and depends on the circumstances. It is impossible to give simple hard and fast rules as there are many factors to be taken into account in a particular situation. Material cooperation (which can sometimes be morally justified) is to be distinguished from **formal cooperation**, which is always wrong. (See definition of formal cooperation above and also the further explanation in the Appendix)
Mental Capacity Act	An Act passed by Parliament in 2005 which reforms the law relating to those unable to take decisions for themselves.
Mental Capacity	See **Capacity**
Office of the Public Guardian (OPG)	An Office established under the Mental Capacity Act which will keep a register of **deputies**, **Lasting Powers of Attorney** and **Enduring Powers of Attorney**, check on what attorneys are doing, and investigate any complaints about attorneys or **deputies**.
Over-treatment	Unwanted or unnecessary medical treatment. Christian faith gives us reason to cherish life, as a gift from God, and also gives reason to accept death, when it comes, with hope in God. It is important to acknowledge that life will come to an end and to prepare for this as well as we can. As death

	approaches, we need to be able to accept this reality and not seek futile treatment. Many people are anxious that they will not be allowed to die naturally and that they will be subjected to unwanted and unnecessary treatment. In this guide we call this 'over-treatment'.
Proxy Decision Taker	Someone who takes a decision on behalf of a person who is unable to take decisions for himself or herself. Examples in the Mental Capacity Act are those appointed as **Lasting power of attorney** or **deputies** appointed by the **court of protection**. All those given such powers by the Act are bound at all times to act in the **best interests** of the person concerned.
Palliative Care	The active care of patients with advanced progressive illness and those at the end of life. Management of pain and other symptoms and provision of psychological, social and spiritual support is paramount. The goal of palliative care is achievement of the best quality of life for patients and their families. Many aspects of palliative care are also applicable earlier in the course of the illness in conjunction with other treatments.
Under-treatment	'Under-treatment' is where a person is not given the medical treatment he or she needs. The life of someone who is sick or dying or disabled must be respected no less than the life of someone who is healthy. One reason that people are anxious about withdrawal of **life-sustaining treatment** is because they fear that sick people will be neglected and not be given the treatment they need. Even if this neglect is at the person's own request, it may be because the person fails to value his or her life.
Willful Neglect	An intentional or deliberate omission or failure to carry out an act of care by someone who has care of a person who lacks (or whom the person reasonably believes lacks) **capacity** to care for himself or herself. Section 44 introduces a new offence of willful neglect of a person who lacks **capacity**.
Written Statements of Wishes and Feelings	Written statements the person might have made before losing **capacity** about his or her wishes and feelings regarding issues such as the type of medical treatment he or she would want in the case of future illness, where he or she would prefer to live, or how he or she wishes to be cared for. They should be used to help work out what is in the person's **best interests**. They are not the same as **advance decisions** to refuse treatment and are not binding.